Gus
Goes to School

First published in the United States by
QEB Publishing, Inc. 2007
3 Wrigley, Suite A
Irvine, CA 92618

ISBN 978 1 84538 896 6

Printed in China

Library of Congress Control Number: 2006038436

Written by Kate Petty
Edited by Clare Weaver
Consultancy by Anne Faundez
Designed by Susi Martin
Illustrated by Maribel Suarez

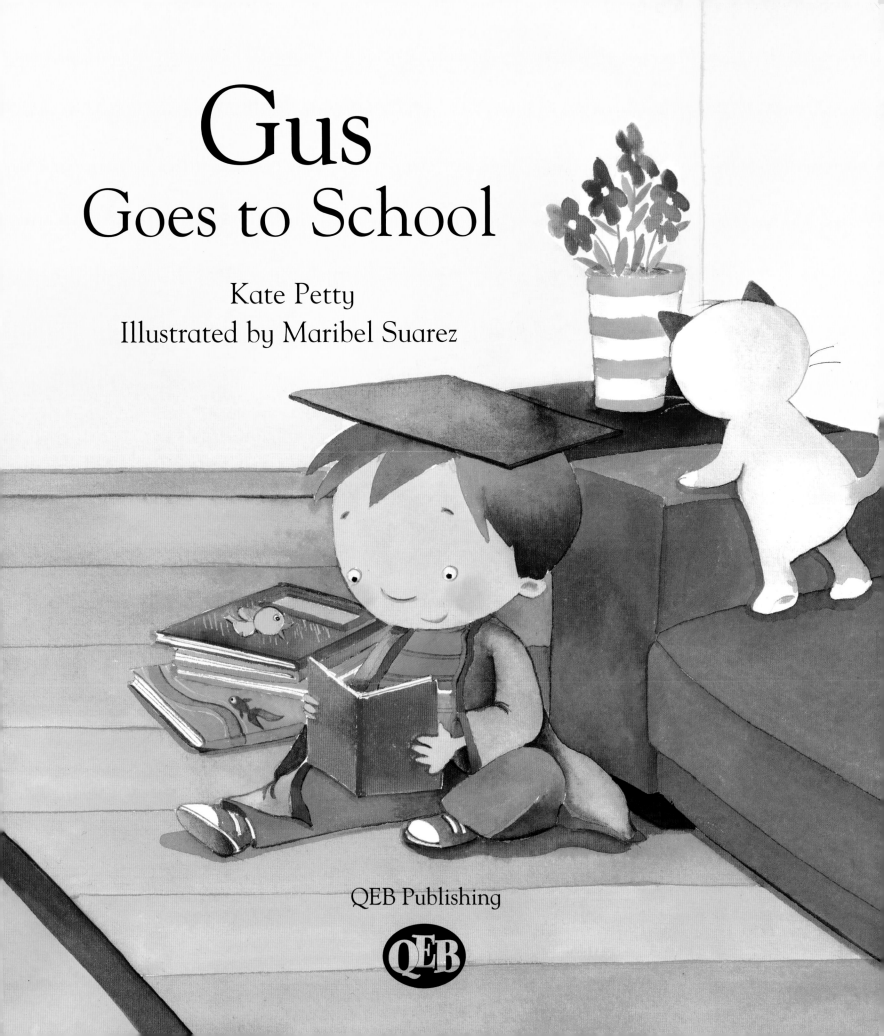

Gus
Goes to School

Kate Petty

Illustrated by Maribel Suarez

QEB Publishing

Monday

It's a whole week until Gus starts school, where his sisters go each day.

Flora and Dora have NO IDEA what he will possibly do now that they aren't at home.

"Have a nice, lazy day!" they say.

"Don't get too lonely with no one to play with!"

As soon as Gus and Mom get home from dropping off the girls, Gus rushes into the living room with no time to waste.

"See you later, Mom," he calls.

Gus puts on his teacher's gown and hat.
"Come along, children. Let's take attendance."

He checks in Mabel the cat and Alf the dog.

The car is very attentive. So is the cushion.

And Ted is probably his star student.

What will they learn today?

It's warm and sunny, and the doors are open.

Gus leads his class outside.

They are going to learn about clouds.

Lions and giants are the best ones.
Clouds that look like many little fish mean good weather.

Then Gus lets his class blow bubbles into the air.

So much science to learn!

Time flies, and soon Flora and Dora are home from school.

Flora trips over the car.

Dora sits on the cushion to watch TV.

"What did you do today, Gus?" they ask.

"Oh, nothing really," says Gus.

But we know better, don't we?

Tuesday

The next day, Gus rushes
into the living room again.

"See you later, Mom," he calls.

He puts on his gown and hat.
There are a lot of books to look
through today. Gus reads a story.

Cushion is a good listener, and soon
Ted will be able to read by himself.

Gus gives him a gold star.

But the car doesn't pay much attention and neither does Alf!

Wednesday

"Don't die of boredom, Gus!" shout Flora and Dora, as they leave for school with Dad on Wednesday morning.

Gus rushes into the garden, putting on his gown and hat. No time to waste. Boredom indeed!

Cooking today.

Mud pies!

All Gus's students love this activity.

It's just Alf who acts a little crazy.
And he encourages the car.

Oh dear! Naughty class!

It's hard work being a teacher.
Gus takes a break for a drink and a cookie
that isn't made
of mud!

"Not too lonely, are you, Gus?" asks Mom. "What have you done today?"

"Oh, nothing really," says Gus.

But we know better, don't we?

Thursday

It's Thursday, and what a day!
All Gus's students are sick!
Mabel…
Alf…

Car, Cushion, and Ted are feeling very sick.

They must have eaten too
many mud pies yesterday.

Gus has to clean up the mess, as well as being the teacher.

Friday

It's Friday. Gus has decided to give his class a day off.
They've learned so much this week!

And he and
Mom have
some important
shopping
to do.

The next Monday is Gus's first full day at school.
He makes a lot of new friends.

They have assembly.

They have classes...

lunch...

playtime...

and a story.

When Gus gets home, Flora and Dora want to know all about his day. After telling the girls about his busy time at school, Gus wonders what his students have been doing all day without him.

Nothing really, he thought...

But we know better, don't we?

Notes for Teachers and Parents

- Look at the front cover of the book together. Talk about the picture. Can the children guess what the book is going to be about? Read the title together.

- Now turn the pages and look at the pictures together without reading the words. What do the children think is happening? Which character do the children think is Gus? Look at the other characters in the pictures. Who might they be?

- Read the story to the children from start to finish. Did the children guess what was happening? Let the children take turns reading pages of the story aloud. Help them with any difficult words they encounter.

- Encourage the children to take turns telling the story in their own words. Remember that creativity is more important than accuracy!

- Discuss starting school and all the preparation that goes into it. How did they feel when they first started school? Were they nervous or excited? Did their feelings change as they settled into school?

- Can the children remember the lessons Gus taught in his classes? What would they like to learn if they could choose anything? Help the children make an imaginary school lesson plan. Include the lessons they would like to learn each day.

- Gus's school is an imaginary one. Imaginary friends can be an important part of children's lives. Do any of the children have imaginary friends? What kinds of things do they do with their imaginary friends?

- Some of the students in Gus's school are a little naughty, but in a funny way. Talk to the children about what constitutes naughtiness.

- Why do the children think Gus stopped teaching school? There are several answers to this question.

- Encourage the children to look closely at Gus's students in the very last picture. What are they doing? What do the children think Gus's students may have been doing while he was at real school?